Little Children's Bible Books

ELIJAH

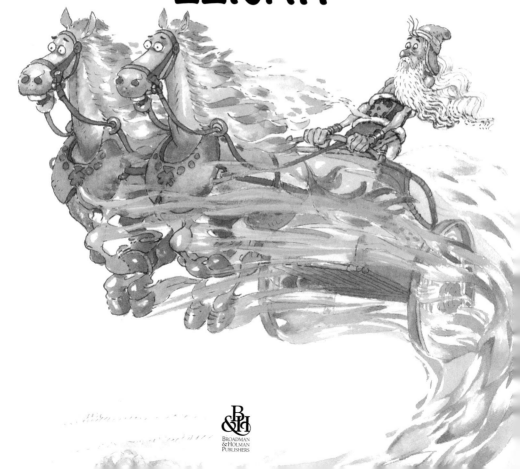

BROADMAN
&HOLMAN
PUBLISHERS

ELIJAH

Published in 2001 by Broadman & Holman Publishers,
Nashville, Tennessee

Text copyright © 2001 Anne de Graaf
Illustration copyright © 2001 José Pérez Montero
Design by Ben Alex
Conceived, designed and produced by Scandinavia Publishing House
Printed in Hong Kong
ISBN 0-8054-2192-0

All rights reserved. No part of this book may be reproduced or utilized in any form or by any means,
electronic or mechanical, including photocopying, recording, or by any information storage and retrieval sys-
tem, without permission in writing from the publisher.

Dedicated to
Pedro Pérez Rollán

Elijah was a prophet. A prophet is some-one who sometimes sees what is going to happen, a see-er from God. He also sees what is happening now. Close your eyes, then open them. Now you can see!

Elijah's job was to warn the people, "Turn back to God!" He even told the king, "As God has told me, not one more drop of rain will fall until I ask God for it!"

Allowing Elijah to do this was God's way of teaching the people of Israel that he was the one, true God. The people needed to SEE that even the rain comes from God. Can you make the sound of rain falling?

The Lord told Elijah to go and hide by a brook near the Jordan River. God took care of Elijah. He sent ravens to bring Elijah bread and meat every day.

Make a sound like a raven, like me. Now flap your arms up and down!

11

Elijah's warning of no rain
came true. Then God sent
Elijah to a village to
ask a widow for food
and water. Although
she was very poor,
she still gave him her
own water, then
offered him her last
handful of flour
and drops of oil.

The widow had almost nothing, yet she shared it with Elijah. God rewarded her by promising to keep her bowl of flour and jar of oil from going empty, as long as there was no rain. What is something you can eat that has flour and oil in it?

For three years no rain fell in Israel. Elijah stayed with the widow all this time. When her son died, he called on God to bring the boy back to life. And God answered his prayer!

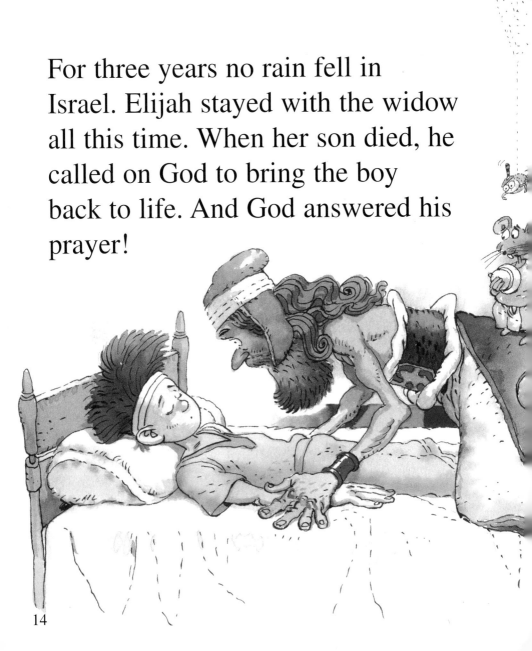

What is something you can pray for? What are some prayers that God answered for you or your family?

15

Elijah listened to God and followed his rules. But the people did not even believe in God. Instead they prayed to false gods. Elijah challenged their priests to a contest.

What is your favorite kind of contest?

17

Elijah saw that many of God's people had turned their backs on God. Because he was a prophet, he SAW people in some of the same ways God saw them. Elijah's job was to bring the people back to God.

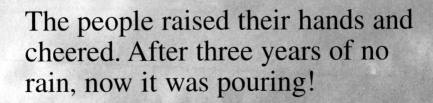

The people raised their hands and cheered. After three years of no rain, now it was pouring!

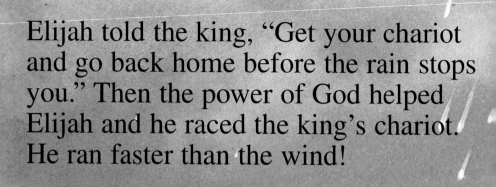

Elijah told the king, "Get your chariot and go back home before the rain stops you." Then the power of God helped Elijah and he raced the king's chariot. He ran faster than the wind!

*Raise your hands high and yell,
"The Lord, he is God!"*

A wicked queen threatened to kill Elijah. So he ran away to the wilderness for 40 days and 40 nights. God sent an angel to bring Elijah food and water so he could make the long journey.

Elijah was looking for God. He felt sad and afraid. Name a place YOU can look for God when you are sad and afraid.

27

When Elijah reached a mountain, the Lord said he would pass by him! But he wasn't in a strong wind. The Lord wasn't in an earthquake, and he wasn't in a fire. Elijah found God in the gentle whispering of the wind.

Move your hands and make a sound like the gentle whispering of the wind.

God gave Elijah a helper. His name was almost the same. "Elisha." Elijah put his cloak on Elisha to show he wanted Elisha to come with him and become a prophet's helper.

Who do you help? What do you do to
help them?

31

When Elijah was an old man, an evil king sent 50 of his soldiers to capture him. Twice! But Elijah called fire down from heaven to protect him.

Do you know how much two times fifty is?

33

Soon after, the evil king fell off the roof of his palace. Now he wanted to know if he would ever get better. Elijah warned the king, "Why don't you trust God and ask him, instead of asking these statues? You will never get better until you trust God."

35

When Elijah was very, very old, God sent horses made of fire galloping through the sky to meet him. Elijah jumped into the chariot of fire they were pulling and went up to heaven.

What a sight that must have been! What sound does a horse make?

A NOTE TO THE big PEOPLE:

The *Little Children's Bible Books* may be your child's first introduction to the Bible, God's Word. This book about Elijah is based on passages from the Bible: 1 Kings 17-19, 22; and 2 Kings 1-2. This is a DO book. Point things out and ask your child to find, seek, say, and discover.

Before you read these stories, pray that your child's little heart would be touched by the love of God. These stories are about planting seeds, having vision, learning right from wrong, and choosing to believe. Pray together after you read this. There's no better way for big people to learn from little people.

A little something fun is said in italics by the narrating animal to make the story come alive. In this DO book, wave, wink, hop, roar, or do any of the other things the stories suggest so this can become a fun time of growing closer.